At the Edge of Town

Poems by Brady Peterson

At The Edge of Town © 2021 Brady Peterson. All rights reserved. Big Table Publishing Company retains the right to reprint. Permission to reprint must be obtained from the author, who owns the copyright.

ISBN: 978-1-945917-67-7
Printed in the United States of America

Cover: Digital illustration by Christopher Reilley
for The Bytesized Studio

Photo: Nellie Peterson

Also by Brady Peterson:
Glued to the Earth
Dust
Between Stations
From an Upstairs Window
García Lorca is Somewhere in Produce

Some of these poems have appeared previously:

The San Antonio Express, The Houston Chronicle: "Ping" and "Something We Miss"

New Texas: "Love and Avocados"

Boston Literary Magazine: "The Ferry," "Diaspora," and "September 7, 2020"

Blue Hole: "Another Day, Another Dollar" (under a different title)

"Making other books jealous since 2004"

Big Table Publishing Company
Boston, MA and San Francisco, CA
www.bigtablepublishing.com

For Butch, Myra, and Bruce

Table of Contents

An Invitation	11
Ping	12
I Come Here Often, He Says	13
Primrose	14
Ghosts	15
Chopin Revisited	16
The Ferry	17
Tailgate	18
Sitting on the Steps of Tor House	20
Flatland	22
Rainy Day Reading	23
An English Garden	24
The Sound of Retreat	26
Ada	28
Ugly Pears	30
Another Day, Another Dollar	31
Diaspora	32
Approaching Thanksgiving, 2020	34
The Great Barrier Reef	35
Bonding	36
Contact	38
Clarity	39
Crows	40
Denim	41
The Resistance	42
Prophecies	43
Everything Happens Here	44
More Than I Hoped For	46
Inventory	47
If Conspiracy Theories Were True	48
Extraction	50

Gravity	51
Goodnight Irene	52
Illuminations	54
A Reckoning	55
Into the Jungle	56
Plots	58
Reading Angela	59
Immediately Green	60
Japanese Sweet Potatoes	61
Legacy	62
Patience	64
Like Breath	65
Playing Christmas Music	66
Not Such a Long Time Anymore	68
A Short Note	69
A Christmas Carol	70
Scripture	71
September 7, 2020	72
September 9, 2020	73
Something We Miss	74
The Billboard Baby	75
The Apple	76
Brown Wasps	78
We Measure What We Lose	80
Using a Whetstone	81
The Secret	82
Napalm in the Morning	83
Things We Don't Talk About	84
'T'is the Season	86
Casting Pearls	87
We Live in Seclusion	88
What Counts	90

What We Do	92
A Journal Entry	95
A Dream World	96
Miscellaneous Jazz	98
November 2008	100
O Come, O Come Emmanuel	101
What We Know	102
Who Is Your Neighbor	103
The Annual Checkup	104
I Fell Yesterday	105
An Old Greek Statue	106
Gray Mornings	108
Real	111
Love and Avocados	112

Notes, references, allusions to other works
About the author

At the edge of town, which was really just two long rows of houses, were two water towers. A big one feeding the plant, and a smaller one feeding the community. As boys, Bruce and I would fire our bb guns at the towers—just to hear the ping of the pellets hitting the metal sides of the tanks. We would pull the trigger—wait, wait—then ping.

An Invitation

We could meet in San Francisco—
at a restaurant on the wharf,
select a table next to a bay window,
perhaps the same table where Merton
and Milosz met that one time.

Angela can order food.
We will drink wine of course.
Look out at the bay.
We need to do this—
while we are still breathing.

We will watch the gulls outside
our window, drink a red wine,
eat bread and olive oil
while we wait for fish to broil.
Talk about the blue of the Pacific.

We connect the ocean
to the rest of the world.

Ping

That love endures seems little more
than words chiseled on a tombstone. We own
the morning, you and I. The house asleep.
A light rain salts the metal roof.

The coffee black. The sky an overcast gray—
so, we simply listen to the sun rising
beyond the tree line. We know it's there,
simply know it's there.

What sound—does love last the day.
Do angels—what are angels anyway but
night wrestlers. Or do they watch over,
lean against the current for us.

Or are they only picking cotton growing
in the black earth. Do they know any better
where and why—could they, if they tried,
wrapped in their immortal boredom.

You are here—the now of it fragile
as fine crystal glass.

I Come Here Often, He Says

Rilke comes to mind, the line about beauty
being the beginning of terror. The moment when you realize
everyone you love—

Berryman tells us Rilke was a jerk, and you find
a certain comfort in the mutterings
of the old drunk.

Miller paints watercolors, hiding out in Big Sur.
Brautigan stands in front of Miller's mailbox
as if to pay homage.

As if Miller's mailbox was the endpoint
of some ancient pilgrimage. You climb the ladder
to ask for a kiss.

Something you missed. Rilke roams the Paris streets,
talking to his angels. Miller gives a grand tour
of his bathroom walls.

Primrose

On first seeing the evening primrose
blooming in my back yard—
I let whatever wants to grow
alone to itself—the yellow sparkling
against the green in a fading light,
I am stunned by the sudden surprise
of such simple beauty.

It is not lost on me in these ancient times
that we are so very—
disconnected from what we call the soul.
As if we had been turned out of paradise—
an old, tired story—and left wandering
like a pack of coyotes over a barren land.

We complain about the youth of today,
how in our time—though the best of it
can be summed up in a pit stop
at a gas station on a dark highway
one Friday after an out-of-town game.

Ghosts

I am losing my feel for the boy—
the one who was me. The one
who took cold showers and climbed
trees, who prayed for roller skates—
captured tadpoles with his cupped
hands and put them in jars
after rains.

He walks from the gym
after basketball practice,
four miles or so to his house.
It is dark, his jacket collar
turned up against the cold.
Hands in his pockets.
He crosses the road with the light.

In the locker room, he watches
two older boys on the team
talk about a girl as they shower.
One of them had wrecked a car
on a back road earlier in the fall.
A friend with him was killed.
Hours before another car came along.

My Latin teacher wept softly
in class the morning after
the accident. *Such a loss,* she said—
At the gym, I watch the older boys
shower and dress after practice.

Chopin Revisited

The storm is coming—
been told for years—knew it true,
but now it's here.

Winds rip shingles from the roof.
Thunder rattles the glass,
Hunkered in the bathtub, muttering—

London bridge is falling down.
What to do.
Grind the last few coffee beans.

Take the key and lock her up.
I never knew a childhood chant
would haunt me

in such a peculiar way.
Lock her up. Lock her up.
I am only four.

I tip the kettle and pour
water almost at a boil
over the grounds.

You appear, cold and wet,
at my door.

The Ferry

We each drink a warm beer and talk
the world into being.
Tanks roll into the city, we scurry
across the rooftop,
wait for choppers to fly us
to an offshore carrier, wait to go home,
though I fear home has been misplaced.

I ride the bus to Dallas.
You head for Seattle, where you intend
to ride the ferry there back and forth
to and from Bainbridge Island.
I walk to Dealey Plaza
and sit on the grass.

At night sometimes, I speak to you
as if we were still young,
as if angels had wings.

Tailgate

One of my old carpenters
and a friend sit on the tailgate
of his pickup parked on a path
next to the river, drinking beer.

I happen upon them
during my morning walk.
My old carpenter gives me a hug
and asks how I've been.

Don't build anymore, do you?
he says. I can smell his breath.
Not for years, I tell him.
Yeah, I don't either, he says.

He gestures with his eyes
to the path winding its way
up the steep hill to the plateau
overlooking the river.

We hear the taps of nail guns
not far from where we are,
nailing studs and rafters,
constructing new homes.

Illegals, he grumbles.
They take all the jobs.
Well, they do show up and work hard,
I tell him. He nods.

Yeah, they do, he admits.
But it is something deeper,
something about how the world
has shifted underfoot.

About how the world—

Sitting on the Steps of Tor House

Catching the sky just right—the thin layer
of clouds a brilliant pink, almost red,
in the minute or two before sunrise,
and I think about Jeffers sitting on the steps
of Tor House and watching the Pacific
crash into the side of Carmel Bay.
There is no wide ocean here, instead
we get the sky.

Last week I watch three vintage airplanes
playing tag over the lake in tight circles.
A man and wife pause in their walk
to watch. "They're having a ball,"
the man says to me. He is a retired master sergeant,
and the tone of his voice tells me he wishes
he could join them, not here and now,
but seventy-five years ago.

As if all things daring or heroic
ended in the aftermath of the surrender.
The emperor announces he is not a god.
Erickson writes memory was lost that day,
wiped clean as one erases the chalk
from a black board—which turns green,
then white.

I want to tell the old soldier the epic warrior
died long before that war, last seen stumbling
in a fog of mustard gas, but I don't think
he would understand or believe me.

Something that wants to cling to the notion
of steel and blood. Something that wants
to cry out—*I am Beowulf.*

How big was the dragon, my British Lit. professor
asks on the final exam. Very big, I answer.
He was not amused.

Here I am toward the end, just now learning
how right Jeffers was, how much we miss,
being so self-absorbed, the flash of cannon fire
lighting our faces. How stupid, Virginia says.

Flatland

I vaguely remember my third birthday—1949.

October, but before the leaves started falling.
My father unloaded a red firetruck from the trunk
of our white Packard, a car he took to Japan,
and sold to a wealthy Japanese businessman.

When my father was shipped back from the war
in Korea to the Army/Navy hospital in Hot Springs,
he bought a new white 1951 Buick.

My mother, brother, and I lived in an upstairs
apartment in a house belonging to Mrs. Wright.
I turned five, had my tonsils removed,
woke up from surgery and threw up
in a stainless-steel bowl waiting for me.

One sunny day, a man left his pick-up running
while he slipped into a bar for a beer.
The truck jumped into gear and took off
down the street. It rammed our shiny white Buick.

A crowd gathered. My mother talked to the police.
She said something about the sun getting into her eyes.

Weeks later, my father bought a new 1952 two-toned
green Buick to replace the white one. Though it had been
repaired, it would never be the same to him.

Rainy Day Reading

He sits barefoot outside in his plastic chair.
It is raining, a light mist really. He could sit in the rain,
but he chooses instead to go back into the house
where he cuddles his books.

Reads Jane Kenyon and Carolyn Forché—
not really companion pieces,
but close enough. They appear on the page
like Crusoe's tiny volcanos,

or the island a mate sees forming
through his binoculars, steaming
in distant waters. Bishop writes
instructions to be posted on the classroom door.

Please continue studying all the Roethke
poems in the Norton Anthology.
She promises to meet the class on the 7th
but dies on the 6th instead.

His desk is cluttered with pages
of a manuscript unfinished,
sentences written in #2 pencil.
Odd, he thinks, his affection for graphite.

An English Garden

Look down from my upstairs window:
the dead brown weeds, stick figures bent
by the wind, the new green winter grass
growing in my old garden—abandoned
some years ago, without much regret.

This working dirt into food.

The deer, the raccoons, the sparrows,
the fire ants, the hideously ugly grey squash bugs
covering the underside leaves of my summer
squash. Tomato hornworms.

I think about trying it all again.
Reconnect with the earth and sun,
dig the ground with a spade
and turn the soil. Pick out the grass roots
with my hands and toss them
into the compost.

Planting tomatoes, basil, onions, and watermelon.
Mustard greens and sweet potatoes.
The old urge whispers in my ear,
but it's still only December.

On my desk: four tiny fat buddhas,
a copy of Tyndale. The buddhas were
a gift. Tyndale introduced to me
by Brett Foster in a workshop seven years past—
we read from the second chapter of *Acts:*

When the fiftieth day was come, they were all
with one accord together in one place.
And suddenly there came a sound from heaven,
as it had been the coming of a mighty wind,
and it filled all the house where they sat.

The fat buddhas grin.

Tyndale is executed—first strangled then burned
for translating the ancient Greek into the vernacular—
the literary mother of modern English.
Tyndale's body is covered with squash bugs.
They crackle in the fire.

Brett Foster dies in three years
from colon cancer. He was forty-two.
We exchanged a couple of emails.
I thought we might become friends—
but I found myself instead drinking a *reposado*
in Las Vegas, New Mexico.
I head down a dark alley—
a crow sits perched on a tree branch.
It speaks to me.

The Sound of Retreat

This is what it is like when you lose a country.
He sips his coffee and looks out the window
at the dreary rain. It has rained for forty days,
it seems. He looks for animals pairing.

It's only the rain.
A grey cloudy drizzle, making it impossible
for the plumber to dig up the collapsed
pipe going from his washer to the septic tank.

It will be $750, the plumber
tells him. Good thing I'm rich, he mutters.
A recurring line he uses at the check out
when buying groceries.

He reads a commentary about the president,
about the takeover of justice—just another brick…
Down the street a neighbor flies the flag
in front of his house—even in the rain.

He remembers learning flag decorum
as a boy, growing up on post, how they stood
attention for retreat every afternoon at five.
How he believed that if he let the flag drag the ground—

just touch the ground.

But that was a time when history mattered—
even if diluted.
No mention of Sand Creek or the Philippines.
Nothing about exemptions for Texas
when Mexico abolished slavery in 1829.

But history mattered, he says as he bends
over to tie his shoe.

Ada

You and I, one evening in Oklahoma,
sat across from one another at a wooden
table on a patio out back and talked
about Bishop's poetry.

Drew offered to buy you a beer,
but you declined. I don't drink anymore,
you said softly. Bishop was a mean drunk,
Mark wrote me one evening, and I believe him.

I have known mean drunks, and Mark knew shit
like that about poets and song writers.
He knew about Neruda's jilted lovers,
about Joni's failure to find the one true

love our mothers told us we would find,
would appear perhaps in a bookstore one day,
and you would just know.
You would feel it in your bones.

You and I were talking about Bishop
sitting in the dentist's waiting room
in Worcester, Massachusetts.
February 1918.

Bishop will be seven in three days.
She hears her aunt cry out,
and in that moment, she falls off the edge
of the world, her aunt and she being one—

not with just each other, but with the naked
women in the *National Geographic*
Bishop was reading. I have a copy
of that issue, Mark tells me.

I have written this before, the waiting room,
falling off the edge of the turning world.

You sit across the table from me,
you being famous. We are waiting
for you to read that evening.
I only know two of Bishop's poems,

I explain. I have read one of your books,
but reading and knowing are not the same.
Knowing is more intimate.
Even then, intimacy is a delicate balance.

One can easily lose touch,
forget an anniversary, fail to notice
or even hear. A poem sits unread
on a shelf too long.

If we were to meet again,
if you remembered me at all,
I would want to tell you I have since
sat with Crusoe on one of his tiny volcanoes.

Later that evening you read your poems
in a large auditorium to much applause.

Ugly Pears

My pear tree grows ugly fruit.
It's November, and the limbs
are weighted down with gnarly
brown spotted yellow pears.

They taste good, but there are too
many to eat—hundreds. Can't give
them away—too ugly. James makes
a syrupy pear base sauce for the Dutch
babies he bakes in an iron skillet.

My father talks to me from the grave
about starving children in Korea.
He fought in that war.
Also, in North Africa and Italy
when he was still just a boy.

The pears ripen and drop to the ground
for the raccoons and hungry possums.

Another Day, Another Dollar

A central Texas morning rises on Wednesday,
just another workday during the pandemic.
Over a million cases in the state so far,
over nineteen thousand deaths.

In El Paso the morgues are at capacity—
what does that mean?
The Lt. Governor interposes
himself into the equation.

Complains about a judge's shut down
order. Come out here and see for yourself,
the judge says. There is a sentiment
expressed that the old should be willing

to die for the good of the economy.
I am old. I breath in the morning
sitting in a plastic chair barefoot
in my front yard.

It is cold, but the sun shines warm
on the side of my face.

Diaspora

You knew a carpenter whose wife
left him for a doctor. She was the high school
beauty, and he was the star running back.
They married shortly after graduating.
One day she wakes up, he tells you during a break.
"What have I done," she says to the ceiling.

Got to give her credit for good sense,
you say. That's true, he admits.
But you should've seen LeRoy chasing
the doctor around the hospital parking lot
with his hammer, another carpenter joins in.
The whole crew laughs.

LeRoy died a few years later
while working a job in Dallas.
Heart attack. He was forty-one.

Joseph was a carpenter, but we don't know
his story after Jesus was twelve.
Joseph, like MacArthur, simply fades from the narrative.
Mary, on the other hand, is present at the cross.

The walls of the second Temple are torn down
by Roman soldiers almost forty years later.
The Jews driven from Palestine.

They rejected Jesus, your hometown preacher
offers as an explanation. They stood up to Rome,
you tell an old war buddy as the two of you drink
a decent *reposado* in a bar in New Mexico.

Approaching Thanksgiving, 2020

Fall in central Texas mostly comes in yellows.
There is the red oak I planted as an acorn
in my front yard, but the red isn't as brilliant
as the ones I saw in Maine the October week
we spent with my aunt after I mustered out of the navy.

We drove through New Jersey and New York
in the 1970 VW bug. Arrived in Norway where a woman
came up to our car when we were getting gas
to tell us she was from Texas—seeing our plates,
she just had to say hello, as if we were lost friends.

I spent an afternoon splitting wood there.
Wore a flannel shirt with the sleeves rolled. Happiest days
always seem physical for me—hiking a mountain
trail in Utah, chopping wood in Maine, riding
my bike across west Texas with my brother.

Eating when hungry—a cheeseburger in Cross Plains,
clam chowder in Trinidad, California.
North of Trinidad we strolled into the old growth forest.
God seemed different to me among the redwoods—
sadder, but a little less angry.

The Great Barrier Reef

bleaches white in the warm Pacific.
The moment has passed us—
We mow our lawns on Saturday morning
as if clipping grass were a sacred duty.
We promise someday, but someday
is a stone.

Tiger wins the Master's. We weep
when he talks about his children
watching him. We weep when Freddy sings
at Wembley, and the crowd sings back.

Another kind of breathing.
Stands barefoot in the cut weeds of his yard—
The round earth falling—falling.

Bonding

There is a New Year's Eve party.
I'm dancing with a girl I just met.
She is seventeen. I am nineteen.
My father would kill you for just
what you're thinking, she whispers
in my ear as we move slowly
to some local band singing "Bring
It on Home to Me."

I am too drunk to care about her father,
but I am also too drunk or too young
or too stupid to know what to tell her.
We dance, and somewhere in the equation
she gives me her shoes. I slip them
into my back pockets.

In the morning I wake in the front seat
of my Chevy. The car is in front of Brian's
house. Brian was driving, I remember
that much. He had taken my wallet
for safety but left the keys in the ignition.
I start the car and drive home.
My father greets me when I try
to sneak in the back door.

Up kind of early, son, he says
I nod and head to my bedroom.
That was probably our closest moment,
and somehow, I knew it.
The girl's shoes still in my pockets.

Contact

I listen to the cars pass by
in front of my house.
Six thirty on a Saturday morning,
not the usual going to the office
crew. Though some may
be heading for work.
Not everyone has Saturday off.

Men are building houses
in the new subdivision—
framers, stone masons, roofers,
electricians, plumbers…
I ride past them on my bike
later this morning.
We exchange nods.

Phatic discourse—
We are here on this round
earth. Later today, it will be hot,
your shirts drenched in a salty
sweat. Water becomes the currency
of the moment. I want to say something
about how you and I—

but I manage only a slight nod
of my head. You nod back.

Clarity

Rain lilies sprinkle the yard this morning:
single stem, six petal, white flowers
that pop up and bloom for a few days
after a good rain.

The wet grass and weeds are ankle deep
around his feet as he sits in a plastic chair—
watches the morning come into being.
Holds himself still in the moment.

I am a statue, he whispers,
made of soft stone. I will sit here
until the wind blows me away
or the next rain dissolves my bones.

Or until he feels the need to pour
a cup of coffee, the coffee
brewing inside in the house.
If the world would only stop.

A blue pickup passes on the road.
The driver honks and waves,
and pulls him back into the narrative.
He raises his hand to acknowledge—

In California, fires rage
up and down the state.
Here, the ground is popping
rain lilies.

Crows

It's one of those evenings when you wish you could sit in a bar at the Algonquin hotel in New York with a friend or two, or maybe in the lobby of LaQuinta in Ada, Oklahoma, or maybe the bar in the Plaza Hotel in Las Vegas, New Mexico and drink tequila or whiskey slowly and talk about poetry and fathers, about the radiation still leaking from the Fukushima reactor or an old lover last seen in Austin, Texas who once loved you dearly but would rather see you dead than see you again, about riding the rails in a '61 Impala one night outside of Abilene, Texas, about boot camp in the winter of 1967. About a Giants try-out camp in Huntsville. About the loss of a child.

Somewhere in the evening you carry the conversation into the head and blubber about how the full moon still gives you pause. You mention the crows in the trees in the alley and how you felt it to your bones—these messengers of death.

Later in the evening, you wander back to the house at the end of the alley. It's been six years, and the house is alone. The back door is unlocked, and you enter. No furniture. No electricity. You make your way back to the bar, but your friends are gone, and the music has changed. You order another tequila, but the bartender, who is the same person who served you drinks at Dee's when you were at Presidio, tells you you've had enough.

You head back up the Ho Chi Minh trail—that's what you called it in those days—spend the night curled around the commode, and you promise God, but you can't remember what it was you promised him.

Denim

The times when you called jeans Levi's
and only wore the ones with a button-down fly—
a story told about caught in a zipper in a public bathroom.
Worn without a belt because your hips were still wider
than your waist.

The taste of a fountain coke and a kiss in the front seat
of your car, a '62 Chevy, at a drive in. Lips warm and moist.
Pick a film, any film will do. *Hud* comes immediately
to mind—Paul Newman turns and grins.

Decades later it is *The Year of Living Dangerously*.
Sigourney Weaver turns and looks at Mel Gibson,
and you instantly know everything important,
every story told.

You are sitting on the union patio
of a major university, or so it aspires to be.
You listen to the sounds and rhythms
of people talking, people who read books.

You drink your coffee black while writing notes
for class. You are reading Baldwin,
but it is much too early in your life to appreciate
what it is to live as a stranger.

Still, you measure the difference between
the loose hanging Levi's—you still wore them then,
and a cup of black coffee.

The Resistance

I am cooking dried chickpeas
in an *Instant Pot*.
Pour in the dried beans and cover
them with water—a little more
than an inch.

The news is on, the leader droning on
about people who hate America.
I turn it off and instead look
for a chana masala recipe
online. Black mustard seeds
popping in hot ghee.

Today we will save the world
by cooking a chickpea casserole.
Tomorrow we will embrace
and talk about children—
or the time we walked
the path next to Town Lake.

Prophecies

The cuff on my morning bath robe dips
into the water as I scrub the baking pan
left over from last night's dinner.
I'm searching for a metaphor—
something about the end of times,
no doubt.

I squeeze as much of the wet
out of the robe as I can, roll the sleeves
up, and continue scrubbing the pan.
Coffee is brewing, Nicaraguan.
I think about Sandino and the US Marines.

Outside the window above the sink,
I watch a cardinal flutter at the bird
feeder. It's Saturday, and I've slept later
than usual. It's November. My poems
are still sleeping upstairs.

Scott warns me against using
the first-person pronoun. Brautigan tells
us about a man who replaced the plumbing in his
house with poetry. In the story the minor poets
inhabit what was once the commode.

An ode to the minor poets.
My robe dips its sleeve into the warm
soapy water. The world ends.

Everything Happens Here

You sit in a plastic chair in your front yard,
bare feet on the cold wet grass, the leaves
on the red oak shimmer in the morning
sun. The day is brittle with November.
Yesterday, you bought a smoked turkey
and sweet potatoes and cranberries,
ran into an old friend—talked again
about children, now grown.

With eyes closed you listen to the sound
of cars passing by, birds tweeting—
the geese migrating south haven't arrived yet,
and you wonder if they will make it this year,
all things normal seem suspended.
Let go of the war in your mind, the poet
whispers. Listen to the birds instead.
Feel the curve of the earth against your feet.

Laura writes she talked to her dead mother
who told her not to worry. No one really dies.
It is one of my fears, you tell her.

You open your eyes. The sun is hiding behind
the oak across the road. Saturday, buzzards
gathered under the tree and fed on the carcass
of a deer run over. Today, they are gone.
The bones of the deer are missing too.

We last left Hans stumbling past the dead
in no man's land—stumbling, stumbling…

It's only a book. The war never happened,
just a story told by a 400-pound man sitting
in the basement of his home, sipping hot chocolate,
typing code.

You leave your perch, the beige plastic chair,
and return to the warm house, remove your knit hat
and slip it into the pocket of your jacket,
remove your jacket and hang it in the closet.
Pour a second cup of coffee, coffee the blood
of a god.

The new baby cries. It's all he knows to do
for now. He is beginning to track people
with his eyes.

More Than I Hoped For

I am not complete, but it would
be beyond foolish
for me to expect—demand
you make me whole.

This is said over coffee
on a morning when the first cold
of the year wraps the country
around us. The rain taps
our metal roof.

We are not the same,
you and I, but we are here
inside this warm house together.

Inventory

Something to ease the stomach—
bread is tempting, but seems to make
it worse. Could be gluten, or perhaps
a *round-up* residue.

Coffee doesn't help, but coffee
is a sacrament—a ritual of divine grace.
I sip it slowly in remembrance.

Grab a handful of cherries
in the refrigerator.
The cherries were on sale this week.

Ripe figs from my tree lie on the butcher-
block table in the kitchen.

If Conspiracy Theories Were True

I sip coffee already cooled in an upstairs room
which is chilly enough for a cashmere sweater—
I wear it as much for the feel of the soft wool
against my skin as for warmth.

I am barefoot though. I tend to go barefoot
in the house year-round. I work out barefoot.
Sit in a plastic chair in my front yard
in the morning barefoot.

Even with frost on the ground, I sit wrapped
in my jacket, gloves, knit cap, but barefoot.
Something about touching my skin to the ground
or to the wooden floors.

There's more, but I am distracted,
sitting in my upstairs room, by the garbage truck
driving past my house. The truck becomes for me
both the expression of honest work and the decline

of our civilization. Civilizations come and go,
I mutter to the windowsill. The four ceramic fat Buddhas
laugh at me. The truck stops. A forked mechanism
grabs the bin sitting on the side of the road and empties

its contents into the truck's belly. The driver
is alone. Two years ago, an additional worker
rode on the back bumper and emptied the bins
by hand. So much for honest work.

My brother and I used to drive our pick-up
to the county landfill, a much better word than dump,
when cleaning out rentals after our tenants left.
Occasionally, we would save a discarded treasure.

Someone once left a forty-pound chrome bar
with an angled edge at the end. I called it the banger
and used it to break up the limestone rock
when I dug post holes for my garden fence.

But most of the stuff left behind was hauled
to the landfill. A woman sitting behind an open window
would eyeball our load and charge us ten dollars,
or was it twenty, I don't remember.

I do remember the rotting smell of the place.
We once dumped a commode left so black
that we chose to replace it rather than clean it.
Carpet saturated with pet urine—bed mattresses.

My brother is resting in a local cemetery now.
Beside him are his wife and daughter. My daughter
is there too, next to a tree.
I rarely visit.

It is early February, and from my window
I can see fire ant mounds starting to appear
in the fields. I have more or less adjusted
to the reality of fire ants.

Extraction

Because he is lost,
not knowing where—frost
on a window glass
gives a rough estimate of when,
though seasons blend here.

I drink coffee black, he says,
as if it would explain, exonerate,
capture the essence. He sings
to the wind whistling outside,
or to someone he loved—perhaps

in a former life—assuming.
The dentist pulls his gold capped
tooth and drops the metal
into a paper envelope. This is yours,
the dentist tells him.

Gravity

They ride in the bed of pickups,
brandishing long rifles,
trigger fingers ready—
flat earthers one might suspect,
eager for the chance to prove—

The yearning need to feel
something, to be something—
beyond their grasp.
To kill if given
the chance.

It's a game, no different
from the ones we played
as boys, hiding behind
tree trunks or parked cars—
Bam, bam, you're dead.

A boy clutches his chest,
falls to the ground.
Stay there, we warn.

We used to shoot at buzzards
with our .22s. when older.
We lay on our backs
in a field feigning dead,
trying to coax the birds into range.
That the bullets fell to the ground
somewhere—

Goodnight Irene

I can lose myself in old photographs,
especially the black and white snapshots
from days before we had television
or even a telephone. We sit on the front porch
of the old house on College Street.
We live in a back apartment, my brother,
my mother, and I.

A man rides his wagon, pulled by a mule,
up the narrow road. The children taunt him.
Children do things like that—mimicking
what they hear at the dinner table,
thoughtless and cruel. I am silent,
but I am among them—
not so innocent.

I am only four, I want to explain.
Eeny, meeny, miny, mo...
How many times did we recite—
picking someone or something,
as if it were chance.
The man keeps his head down,
bearing the weight on his shoulders.

The photograph of him is not on paper,
but etched permanently in my brain.
I do not know you, old man, I say.

You must be dead by now, gone
with everyone else. Gone with the men
who played baseball in the open
lot across the street from our house.

My brother and I sit on the front porch
and sing "Goodnight Irene."
We wait for my father to come home
from the war. There was no college
in that small town—just the street.

Illuminations

When we die, are we relieved
of the need to fix things,
or do particulars follow us
into some Karmic afterlife.
No reward for a life well lived,
just the gnawing requirement
to fix shit.

Troublesome is the possibility
of having to do it again
as someone else with memory erased—
come back as a lizard, or a buzzard,
or if extremely unlucky, as Cleopatra,
asp clutched to her breast.
We loop through time.

Discover ourselves acting character parts
in a sci-fi novel written hastily
with a #2 pencil in a coffee shop,
the coffee bitter black and cold.
To fix something broken,
a line poorly spoken, salvage
the ruins of an old civilization.

Scurry over a kitchen counter-top
at night. The light flickers on, then off.

A Reckoning

It isn't that we recognize
assassins too late.
We've known them all along.

We just don't care,
no matter how we play
it when the rooster—

We didn't know, we will say,
shrug our shoulders, our hands
turned up in hapless surrender.

We didn't know—honest—
hoping beyond hope
there is no God, no hell.

Into the Jungle

When a people sink into the heart of madness,
can they be redeemed? If so, at what price?
If so—

Clarity becomes a sentence without a verb.
Language folds like burning paper.
We look for grace in the ash.

I am reading the letters
between Robert Lowell and Elizabeth Bishop,
you write me on a Saturday morning.

I love hearing about what you are reading,
I write back, as if someone reading anything
means sanity still exists somewhere.

Elizabeth worked three months on one poem,
you say. Robert Lowell worried constantly
about not having enough money.

There is a copy of *The Cantos* on my desk,
I want to tell you, but that might obligate
me to read them.

An American summary. A stump speech
given on a Wednesday—was it Wednesday—
in front of the Tower when I was a freshman.

I can show you a small crater in the concrete
between pillars on a wall just north
of Parlin Hall made just two years later.

What? Never mind.

The heart has always been there,
upstream, in the jungle. On an August
day in the middle of a university campus.

When I returned to the university
after the navy, I found the weekly stump
speaking had been discontinued.

Plots

No doubt, we will cry to heaven,
but God will not help us—
we should know that.

However petty or mean—
God or us—mean being a norm.
Let me not be one, he prays—

of the many, or the few
for that matter.
What else is there?

Who the hell knows,
he grunts and heads out
to his garden where he digs dirt

with a spade. I will plant
beets and turnips, he thinks.
Melons and beans.

Reading Angela

Give us our God back, the crowd
urges in Angela's poem,
but who—he shimmies down
the wall of a narrow canyon
to the stream bed.
His hip aches.

Not God, but our—
Clarence plays the saxophone
so sweet one hears the stark
truth of its beauty.
He crosses the stream.
Steps into the cold water.

Immediately Green

Rain is sacred here
where the ground stays dry
and cracked much of the year.

I joke about falling
into one of the wide fissures
and disappearing into the earth.

When it rains, the fissures snap shut,
gullies fill with rushing water,
and low water bridges become death traps.

The brown grass turns immediately green
during the storm. That's hyperbole—
but this is a land of hyperbole.

Japanese Sweet Potatoes

Twice today, the impulse was to walk across the road
and check on you only to remember the house
was empty. "You still alive," I used to ask.

Well, shit—I mutter this to the dying oaks
in my front yard. Two oaks at your house
are now showing signs of decline—

splotches of brown leaves. Last week,
a neighbor's tree dropped a limb on his chimney,
breaking off a couple bricks.

This morning, I watered your tomatoes
and sweet potatoes. Two purple blossoms
peered up through the wide green leaves.

Sweet potatoes are in the morning glory
family, I tell no one in particular.

Legacy

Try to remember when your father was kind.
He was that way sometimes, when he wasn't drinking,
your brother would say—*easy to blame the booze*.

"He drinks too much," your grandmother tells you.
The two of you talk on the back porch.
Her deafness, a residue of childhood measles,
causes her to get most of the conversation wrong.

Lives in a world apart. Speaks softly
as if to compensate. Extends the vowels
and gestures, raising an imagined glass
to her lips.

"He drinks too much," she almost whispers.
But did drink bring on the dark moodiness
or could it be the other way around.

And aside from the visits when you are dreaming,
the old man is gone—dead going on thirty-six years,
so why not just let it go. "Why cling to old baggage,"
Angela says, really talking about Hank, not you.

Your father shows up in your dreams, risen
from the grave. You wake, roll out of bed,
not wanting to go back to sleep.

This deep yearning you have to be free
of him. So much so that if heaven required
a reunion, you just might choose hell.

You roll out of bed, and after visiting the head,
brew a pot of coffee, grinding the beans
in your burr grinder, one of several luxuries
you afford yourself.

"If it wasn't for your father," his cousin
tells him at a family get together—
a great aunt's funeral, he thinks, "you
and your brother wouldn't have a pot to piss in."

His cousin draws a certain satisfaction
in having made that declaration.
A reflex smile, when one doesn't really want
to engage yet another asshole.

Patience

An old fisherman
sits in a small boat—the calm
open water of the lake, his beer
turning warm. Only a few swallows
in, more ritual than thirst.

He more or less watches the line
where it meets the water
and doesn't really care if the fish
are biting or not. Holds the rod
in his left hand. As close to the Buddha
as one dares—

His thinking drifts—his father, uncle,
and brother are in a boat fishing
on the Brazos river—a December morning.
It is so cold the eyelets of their rods
freeze solid with ice. The men shiver. Miserable.
Yet keep fishing, keep hoping the sun

will appear any minute and warm
their stiff fingers. Pour coffee
from a red thermos just to watch
the steam rising from their cups.
They are dead now—all three.

Like Breath

It's easily knocked from its perch
on the bookshelf. Falls face down
on the hard wood floor—lies there
while you retreat to the kitchen
to put on a fresh pot.

The ritual of grinding beans,
measuring water. Earlier you loaded
your laundry in the machine and started
the wash cycles. An old friend severs
ties unexpectedly without explanation.

You want to ask why, but decide
instead to let it go. You pour a cup
of black coffee and return to your desk.
Read a poem by Gertz, then another
by Hall. Sink into the words.

Soaked with sugar from Thanksgiving
pecan pie and whipped cream,
yams with toasted marsh mellows,
you promise to reset your diet,
take a long walk along the river.

Friends come and go, you tell yourself.
Like breath.

Playing Christmas Music

The smell of burning leaves,
the drive over a rutted gravel road
the miles between Fulton and Okay—
you've written this before, how the cold
floors of your grandmother's house stung
your feet in the morning.
Biscuits and strawberry preserves,
eggs over easy, coffee with milk and sugar
in a tall glass.

Myra talks about place and story—
and song. You listen to the harmony
of voices. The memories fold themselves
into the leaves of an old black page
album with the photographs of people who knew
how to churn butter from milk.
The faces of people you knew
but don't remember. A great aunt
sits in a chair on the front porch
of her house. Your grandfather parks
his Ford in her front yard.

Man, she calls him.
She spits snuff into a tin can.

You are nine in the scene, home for Christmas,
though home was just a word your mother used,
more like home base in a game of hide and seek.

In the car, so much of the world seen from the car,
your mother drives and tells the stories of being young,

about moving to Texarkana after graduating high school—
during the war. She was engaged to two men when
she married your father, she says, though
not really engaged. I never said yes, she explains.
They just assumed. Still, there was a ring.

I had scholarship offers, she says, but girls
didn't go to college. She wanted to move to New York
and become a reporter. She didn't really want to marry
anyone. But there was the war.

There were guns in the house one assumed were loaded—
not like the assumptions of my mother's suitors.
I now have one of the pistols, a Colt .44-40 special,
but the Savage single shot twelve gauge,
the one I carried into a field one December day,
is missing.

Not Such a Long Time Anymore

Lincoln in a photograph stands above the crowd,
tall, angular, the Wilt Chamberlain of his era,
surrounded by shorter squatty lesser men.
Do we see him in a photograph or is it the slippery
memory of a description one reads in a poem.

There is the account of the second inauguration
published in a textbook for the Confederate schools
where the police spend much of their effort
dragging a lunatic from a tree—an extended metaphor
no doubt. Lincoln was not loved in the South.

Edna swims from the Louisiana shoreline into the Gulf
toward Cuba, a recurring motif for me.
Castro greets her in Havana, a cigar in his teeth.
Here Edna will be recognized and honored,
he openly declares. But Fidel is a baseball man at heart,

the art of the curve is his only love.
Che asks for tobacco from a guard, a dying wish granted.
A brooding storm off the coast, the surf swelling—
we are left wondering what is real.
Who was Eichmann, Mickey Mantle, Marilyn…

Lincoln, if he existed, died eighty-one years
before I was born. Not such a long time anymore.

A Short Note

It snowed seven inches more last night,
she writes, filling the prints left by her grandchildren
during their last outside visit—wearing masks.

Here I watch the grass grow as I sit barefoot
in my yard. Saturdays one hears the sound
of mowers doing their work.

Robins passed through weeks ago, though
we did have that three-day freeze
when the water main burst and we used

melted snow to flush our commodes.
But the pear trees are popping buds now,
and henbits will soon cover the ground

with their tiny purple-pink blossoms.

A Christmas Carol

We are like children of mobsters
growing up in mahogany homes,
believing we are innocent
of the fathers' sins.

We eat Big Macs and fries,
stare into each other's dull cow eyes.
Sooner or later though we join the firm,
the only business we know.

But for now, we decorate the tree
with ornaments made with hand blown glass.
The birth of Christ, the baby swaddled
in a manger.

Do you renounce Satan?

The last scene where Michael
becomes Godfather. *Do you renounce Satan?*
Michael being the cold blooded badass
we, in our heart of hearts, admire.

Marlin bloated, with his cheeks
stuffed with wads of cotton, dies in the garden.
Do you renounce Satan?
I do.

Scripture

We read where the rich are jumping
line to get the covid vaccine,
tomorrow's promise.

Why expect less—
here where money is God.

Explains in part why a grifter
is hailed as the chosen one.

Self-proclaimed: "I am
the chosen one."

A Monday morning
when crows roosted
in the trees outside our home.

The shiny black birds—
messengers of death.

God simply favors the rich,
don't you see.

September 7, 2020

My fig tree would have made Jesus proud
this summer, producing hundreds of juicy
brown fruit, sweet on the tongue,
picked and eaten from the tree.

Its broad green leaves, its insatiable thirst
for water in a land more and more drought
prone. I empty my two large rain barrels
into its roots, trickle the water just so.

My pear tree on the other hand
produced no fruit this year. I've been told
freezing days during winter are important
for the tree to blossom in spring.

My sweaters were taken from their plastic
bags and worn once each. Or twice maybe.
Whatever, it doesn't get cold much here
anymore. But it does get hot.

It rained yesterday, for the first time
in forever. Rain is hope.
It comes now and then—like elections.
I walk outside and stand barefoot on the wet earth.

September 9, 2020

Rain today, for the third or fourth day
in a row. I try to remember if it's Wednesday
or Thursday. Losing track would be bothersome
if I still drove to my office each day—
I once had an office. Filled with books,
student essays stacked on my desk.
A love seat where I napped
in the afternoon when I found myself
reading the same sentence again and again.
Now I don't really care if it's Wednesday.

I had planned to haul the dirt from my brother's
garden to mine, wheelbarrow at a time—
a kind of cross fit training. But the rain,
turning dirt to mud, delays that chore.
God, how we need the rain.
I watch from my upstairs room, a tower
at the west end of my house, the gutters
pouring water into rain barrels.
A squirrel scurries across a power line
then jumps into a cedar.

In the room below me, I hear my wife
talking to our granddaughter via computer,
helping her with her online classes.
Our granddaughter is six and is learning
to read. The ordinary passing on of knowledge.
The tone of my wife's voice so patient,
so filled with today spilling into tomorrow.

Something We Miss

A list of ordinary things—bumping
into someone you knew in high school
at the grocery store. You still see the outline
of her face—pretty still, if pretty matters anymore.

Something she wrote in your junior yearbook
you remember without having to dig it from the bottom
of a backroom shelf. *Maybe we can try again
next year.* But next year had its own plans.

You pause among the asparagus, each holding onto
your shopping cart—seems an appropriate setting.
Jane Kenyon calls the asparagus shoots
rising from the spring mud Lazarus fingers.

Kennedy was gunned down the next November,
a hundred years ago or more. And now here
you find yourself hunkering down, hiding from
something too microscopic to see.

Now you order your groceries on-line.

The Billboard Baby

We drive the desert in your old copper brown Datsun,
the windows down, an ice chest in the back seat,
before they finished the interstate
at Ft. Stockton and Phoenix where we drive
through the outskirts west of the city,
pull in at a truck stop complete with showers
for weary drivers. I buy a cup of coffee.

It's been years. I wonder if the gas station
is still there, if it survived the completion of the highway
which takes us through a downtown tunnel
funneling traffic away from what was once
an ideal spot for a truck stop.

We drive past the billboard baby.
It is smothering hot in the car. We rub pieces
of ice from the chest on our bare legs,
but it doesn't help.

The mountains look like sleeping giants, you say.
Old gods from another world lying face up
toward the sky as if waiting
for some space craft
to take them home.

The Apple

The sin of the poet is to know—original
in its complicity with the serpent, the one
in the garden, the staff of Moses, the bronze
image—to look on it is to be healed,
messenger of gods, companion to the underworld—
good from evil.

She sighs.

Once you know, it's too damn late.
Sweat of your brow. You work dirt into food
with your hands. Chisel stone into the images
of a lover. Pick a flower and press it to your nose.
You pose for the photographers as you step
out from a black limo onto the red carpet.

Red and black.

There is no turning back. You've read
too many books, listened to the blues being played
in a back room somewhere, eaten meat seared
over an open fire, baked bread in a stone oven.
Churned butter with your calloused hands.
Held a dying child in your arms.

He cries

out to the God he no longer believes
listens or cares. Bears the burden of a thousand
years, a single lifetime—steps from the shower
clean but not innocent. But then to hang
onto innocence once it is thoroughly lost
is to become a monster.

Baldwin said that.

She knows it to be true. That's the sin,
delicious in its intent. To step out of a shower,
skin tingling clean. He remembers when
water—the smell of honeysuckles in summer.
Somewhere there's a boy sitting on the back
steps of a house no longer there.

Brown Wasps

It has rained for three days
after a summer long drought,
and my dead grass, like Lazarus—
to say like Jesus would be sacrilege—
rises up from the ground green.

I will need to mow it.
I say grass, but it's mostly
weeds, the distinction
being one of desire.

This mowing fetish
we have always baffles me.
My wife says it's because
of snakes. Snakes hide
in the high grass.

A brown wasp crawls on the screen
outside my window, peering in.
I get lost in one of Loren Eiseley's
essays. Teaching English does that.

I am Eiseley, planting a tree
with his father, then returning
years later to see it full grown
only to discover it gone.

We are like brown wasps
clinging to a wet nest in winter,
Eiseley tells us. I have a riding mower,
I tell him.

We Measure What We Lose

You write a poem yesterday, with pen and blue ink—
not the one you intended, those words dancing
on the fringes, but something less.

Better than watching news, or reading posts
from old high school buddies who hiss their hatred
drowned in syrupy sarcasm.

You look up the word glom. It doesn't mean
what you thought. You like the sound though.
Glom—to steal.

The poem lies naked on the page,
nothing particularly beautiful or grand—
a little bitter with melancholy.

A growing sadness over the loss
of something you remember existing,
perhaps only in the cracks of the story.

I will not give into it, you tell yourself—this sadness
which aches to the marrow of your bones.

Using a Whetstone

I am sharpening knives today,
a way to hide from the current cultural insanity.
I am just now learning the technique. I use a whetstone,
try to hold the knife steady, feel for the burr.
The knives emerge if not razor sharp, sharper.
I am told that practice will make me better.

The boredom of the pandemic,
growing old, feeling the cold breath of death
on the back of my neck has created in me a desire
to acquire a new skill. Develop better hand eye
coordination, create new muscle memory,
mind flexibility.

As if one might actually grow old gracefully,
not as in calmly accepting the inevitable,
but in a gritty defiance to the planned
obsolescence of the human mind and body.
It's a war one cannot win, I know.
But what else should one do with his time.

The old Greek term *arête*—Pirsig and his
motorcycle maintenance trip to Montana,
the Chautauqua. My son-in-law tells me
that skinning a pineapple this afternoon
was almost easy with the sharpened knife.

The Secret

Want is the pathology of the rich,
the poet explains as he pours
the coffee beans into the grinder.
Heats the water.

It's not how much they have,
that pleases them, don't you see.
Their worth is defined instead,
by the things you lack.

Napalm in the Morning

Outside HEB, you wait while your wife
goes in to buy a head of cabbage
she had forgotten to put in her cart
earlier that morning. "It is hard to make
slaw without cabbage," she explains.

A silver pickup pulls in next to you.
It is not a work truck—one can tell
the difference. A man in his forties,
or maybe early fifties, gets out.
Strapped high on his hip is a holster—
black with a black handled pistol.

You wonder if you should follow
him inside. For what—to die in your wife's
place if necessary. Only she emerges
as he enters. You imagine the shootout.
You throw cans of soup,
a Jedi weapon.

Your wife climbs into the car unaware,
happy to have her cabbage.
You lay bleeding on the grocery
store floor.

Things We Don't Talk About

Don't write in first person,
a friend advises, as if ego
could be overcome or erased
by altering pronoun case.

I chase away night demons
by waking early and refusing
to go back to sleep.
I am awake in a dark house.

It is cold. I start the coffee and pull
the curtains back in my front room.
The sun is an hour away.
Even now, the morning traffic

has started to pick up, headlights
and the hum of tires on asphalt.
I pour a cup of coffee, tap my keyboard,
waking the screen.

I read a personal email from an old student
asking for editorial help. Do I charge
for my work, he asks. I junk the rest.
On Facebook, for some reason I search

out an old friend, something I do once
a year, and read where he died suddenly
last spring. His niece doesn't say how.
Heart attack, covid-19, a bullet to the head…

So many are dead now—old friends.

I scribble a note to his niece about teaching
with him in '84, about drinking Shiner Boch
on the student union patio every Friday—
three of us, where we discussed serious matters:

Mary Shelley's maiden name, Fidel Castro
and Edna Pontellier—whether she made it to Cuba
or not, George Meade at Gettysburg.
If there was a better beer than Shiner Boch.

This was in 1984, before the micro-brewery explosion.
I didn't tell her, my friend's niece, about his seeing
two sisters at the same time and the evening
one showed up at his house with a gun.

'Tis the Season

I lose track of the days,
he says. I am not happy about it.
I miss an appointment with a friend—
more than once, this has happened.

Monday, Friday, Wednesday, November—
It rains and the wipers squeak,
smearing the windshield like my memory
when I drive the boy we call our stepson
to a parking lot in Temple where he meets
the UPS driver. A Christmas-season-
part-time job.

He will text me when it's time to pick
him up, he says. It's not raining too hard
to walk, I tell him. I am teasing, but part
of his brain calculates the time it will take
to walk eight miles—in the rain.

At home, I read Forché—the scene which becomes
her poem. The colonel leaves the room.
He comes back in holding a sack. From it he spills
human ears on the table. Write your poems
about that, he says—El Salvador.

I feel it could happen here.
For the first time, I feel the cold reality
of that possibility, and I can't keep track
of the days anymore.

Casting Pearls

Two men knock on my door and invite me to worship
at their local church. One wants to engage me,
asks if I had ever had that moment when I understood
I was a lost sinner who could be saved only by the blood
of Jesus Christ.

I am wearing a mask. They are not.
A political stance or perhaps an act of faith in the age
of the pandemic. I want to tell them my uncle, a Baptist
preacher, just died from covid. But I am instead silent
in the face of his question.

At the core of the inquiry is the insistence
that each of us, that all of humanity, is wretched
and deserving of hell. That all of living
was some cosmic game played out to fix a flaw
in the system, but part of the grand design.

Says something about the design, don't you think?
Don't know if I said that aloud or if I simply looked
at the two men without responding.
I could sense that one of the men was not comfortable
talking to me.

We Live in Seclusion

A new lexicon—like a bradykinin storm
which increases vascular permeability—
blood vessels start to leak everywhere
in the body. The lungs fill with fluid.
Another new word—hyaluronic acid (HLA).
My daughter tells me there is no "d"
when she hears me struggle to pronounce it.
I say it again. You're still saying it with a "d",
she tells me. My eyes and tongue
don't coordinate.

The increased production of HLA
is another dirty trick of the virus.
HLA absorbs more than a thousand
times its weight in fluid. In the lungs,
it works to create a hydrogel.
Your lungs become Jell-O.
Even the ventilators—

Sally Ball tells us in her poem 'Slope"
that oxygen is unremarkable
until it's threatened.
Breathing is easy, until it isn't.

I watch her struggling to breathe
in a different context. Her eyes focus
on mine. I tell her everything will be okay,
but she can't get the precious oxygen
into her blood quickly enough.

I hold her hand and talk about angels
being in the room, as if angels
could breathe for her.

As much as I may wish some people dead,
a flaw in my character, I don't wish
them to drown with lungs full of Jell-O.

What Counts

My rain catcher is tilted like Pisa.
It needs to be leveled, so I empty
the 250 gallons of rainwater, or most of it,
move the barrel from its leaning perch,
then pull the four cinder blocks from the soft,
muddy earth.

I spread several five-gallon buckets
of clay gravel—never mind why I had
the buckets of gravel sitting against my house
for a few years now—on the uneven ground.
I tap the gravel flat, then test it
with a level.

The bubble floats dead center.

I need to do one useful thing a day
to keep the devil away.
It's a notion inflicted upon me
during childhood. Useful becomes
the operative word.

What counts and what doesn't
is something I instinctively know,
but couldn't explain by any set of norms.
Paying the bills counts. Mowing the lawn,
installing a new LED light fixture,
painting my deck, even planting tomatoes.

Reading doesn't count, nor writing poetry—
nor does teaching, I don't think.
I didn't make the rules. I just know them.
Rules imposed upon me by a man
who joined the army at fifteen
to escape the poverty of picking cotton.

The tedium of certain kinds of work
become the measure of one's worth.

I use leverage to place the rain barrel
back into place under the gutter spouts.
I think a couple years of therapy
might relieve me of this need to do
one useful thing a day.

But I am comfortable with the ritual.

What We Do

Whether right matters here in the room
or not, whether your mother raised you in love
or left you in a basket on a doorway step
on a snowy day in Nebraska,
whether you ate pancakes and maple syrup
for breakfast or simply drank a cup
of coffee made from beans grown in Nicaragua—
you prefer Nicaraguan coffee, probably
because you like the feel of the word
on your tongue—whether you watch the circus
on the flat screen or hike the sliver of wild
across the road and down the small canyon
below your house—yesterday, a buck snorted
at you, a leaf fell gently to the ground, the path
covered with yellows and browns—whether you believe
your voice matters or not, you bear witness
because it is what God expects.

We are the eyes, the ears of the world.
The buck snorts at you, the leaf flutters
to the ground, the coffee bean is picked by hand
somewhere distant, perhaps another time
in history, the mystery of Sandino.

You testify before the panel of the walking dead.
I am alive, you tell them. I can still taste the sweet
in a watermelon and in a kiss tenderly given.

I dance to the music of Clifton Chenier
and Piazzolla—barefoot in the grass of my front yard.
People drive by. Someone in a white pickup honks
and waves at me. I wave back.

I see you, the poet whispers in your ear.

I want you green, young García Lorca sings
from the grave. Was he ever not young.
Verde que te quiero verde.
You listen to the rhythm in the voices
of men when you walk by the construction site.
You want to tell them you admire their work.
You once worked lumber in a yard, pulling boards
from bins, loading them in bundles on flatbed trucks.
Your hands calloused, your forearms knotty.

You once swam naked in the Gulf
with your first wife and another couple.
Climbed the steps of the Lincoln Memorial,
rode the elevator to the top of the Empire State Building,
and it didn't matter it was no longer the tallest
building in the world, because it was still
the Empire State Building.

Rode your bike from Abilene to Belton
when Ford was president. Ate cheeseburgers
at a Dairy Queen. Worked the Republican convention
in Austin in '64 where you met John Tower
and George the Senior. A baby elephant shakes
his body and pisses on the floor.

Duke Ellington's band plays in the basement
party that night, and you were taught something
about the true nature of Democracy,
though it was years in the learning.

The world was never right, you realize. But then you
remember your grandmother almost running
to the car to greet your family when you arrived
for Christmas. The joy in her face.

So you tell the committee that right matters,
that every god damn breath, every note
in the song, every step a young couple and their child
take walking from El Salvador or Honduras
to the Rio Grande—you watch a man lay stone
for the walls of a new house—all of this matters,
don't you see.

A Journal Entry

I warm up with my two-pound Indian clubs.
Then I work out with the kettlebells without repeating sets,
doing a different exercise, going from one to the next,
for forty minutes. Maybe not an approved method,
but fun to do. I throw in sandbag squats and barbell
dead lifts for extra credit.

Before my kettlebell workout, I sit barefoot
in my plastic chair in my front yard and meditate.
The sun is up and bright, but the wind is cold.
I wear my jacket. I probably don't take my meditations
seriously enough as I sip coffee during the process.
For me it isn't so much a mystical journey
as it is just paying attention to details.

It works for me. So does hiking in the canyon.
In the canyon, I am only a few hundred yards
from the subdivision houses, but I still find it wild.
I lose myself in the trees. I step over a stream.

I plan to spend the afternoon reading Barry Lopez.
I am embarrassed that I didn't know him until last month
when he died. Mark responded to his death
by telling everyone to read *Arctic Dreams*,
and since Mark is my main reading guide, I order
the book immediately.

A Dream World

He reads a Canto—or part
of one, immediately lost
in the dreamy world

of the fascist—insane
declared, a ploy to forestall
prison, though they did cage

him outside in the elements
until the ploy became real.
He howls at the rain—the pain.

A traitor being the true
nature of the poet,
the poet being true

only to the voices
whispering into the back
of his skull.

Angels, devils—he doesn't know,
only trusts to his luck—
blind.

Where were they, the banker
and the wild man looking a bit
like John Brown at Harper's Ferry,

but writing poems when cars
replaced horses—the shit scoopers
losing their livelihood.

The blacksmith too.
His wife cuts his hair,
depriving the old barber

who closes the door
to his shop, sweeps the floor
one last time.

Miscellaneous Jazz

I look at a photograph of you standing in front
of some railroad tracks. Across the tracks a couple of artists
are working paint onto their easels. The Monterey Boat Works
serves as backdrop.

You are wearing my navy work jacket and a pair of shorts.
A leather purse purchased in Mexico hangs from your shoulder,
the leather aged a dark brown. You stand in a half-turn
Venus de Milo pose, your long legs stretch to your sandals.

It is summer 1977, ten years after I attended language school
on the peninsula. We drove up the coast the day before,
because I wanted to show you my favorite spot in the entire world,
the place Brautigan called the beginning and end of the Pacific Ocean.

Later that day, we walked the streets of Carmel.
In my novel, we then drove down the Pacific Coast Highway,
climbed one of the hills in Big Sur, and made love.
That part was fiction. I did climb one of those hills,
but it was with a navy friend, a submariner I briefly knew.

The photograph is now tucked under the glass on my desk along with busines cards, most of them long out of date, and three other pictures. One of my parents' liquor store, one of my father and Uncle Huey in Korea, and a wallet size picture of one of my daughters.

November 2008

We were in New York attending a poetry
convention. The city full of energy, Obama t-shirts
for sale on the streets everywhere. I wanted to buy one,
but was more a 10K run t-shirt kind of guy.
Still, it felt as if we as a nation—

The first morning we met outside White Horse Tavern,
a small group set to tour the village. A young professor
from Fordham our guide. We walked the sidewalks.
She pointed out where poets had lived and died.
Earlier, I had eaten a bowl of oatmeal at a small
cafe. The sound of clattering dishes from the kitchen.

O Come, O Come Emmanuel

When this is over, a more and more commonly uttered
phrase beginning any talk about future plans…
I listen to Pentatonix sing Christmas songs as I watch
Christmas Eve morning come into being.
I haven't listened to much Christmas music this season.

I hear my grandson's voice in another room.
He is playing with sounds the way very young children
do. My grandfather was 42 when I was born.
I was 73 when my grandson was born. I count that way,
marking the calendar. My grandfather was 58 when he died.

That I am still alive to see my grandchildren
is not lost on me. It's Christmas Eve, just another day
in so many ways. I step outside barefoot. It is 32°,
but the air is calm. My bare feet adjust to the ground.
A collage memory trick, the ghosts of Christmases past.

What We Know

The freeze, the water main breaking—without water
for three days. But we at least had power.
Some across the state froze to death in their homes.

James and I go out back and crack through
the crust of ice with our shovels,
dig out the snow underneath,
and put it in five-gallon pails to be melted
and used to flush the commodes.

My daughter reports the produce bins at HEB
are empty. The same for the bread aisles.
We do have flour and buttermilk for biscuits,
a modest supply of food, a few gallons of drinking
water. We are fine for now.

A temporary glitch in the equation,
we tell ourselves. Still, I have dreamed this before,
only I had hoped it was just a dream.

Who Is Your Neighbor

I give a small donation to AOC's Texas relief fund.
She is trying to support a Houston food bank—
eventually collects over five million dollars for the cause.
I post my effort on Facebook which goes against scripture,
but I post it, nonetheless. An old high school buddy
responds with an angry emoji.

What kind of asshole would be angry with my giving
to a food bank? I mutter. But then I know what kind.

AOC, who knows her life is in danger maybe anytime
she is in public, goes to Houston to help deliver
food to the hungry, to the desperate. She lives in danger
because, unlike Prufrock and unlike the Texas senator
who flees to Cancun during the freeze, she dares.

The Annual Checkup

I go to the doctor, and after looking at my charts,
she tells me I have a 25% chance of having a major
cardiac event in the next ten years. I like the way
she says cardiac event. As if someone had smoked
brisket all day for the occasion.

In ten years, I will be 84, I tell her and decline
her offer to medicate me. Yes, she confirms,
your age is the major contributing factor.
My blood work was actually better than it was
two years ago.

I give her a copy of one of my books. She acts
interested, and maybe she is. I tell her I will see her
next year if I am still alive. If I am still living in Texas.
I have been meaning to move to California
for forty years, I tell her.

I Fell Yesterday

I tripped on a yoga block left in the middle
of the room and fell face first into the edge
of a chair.

Thoughts of my friend Ron falling in his living
room and breaking his neck immediately came
to mind as I lay on the floor.

But aside from being momentarily stunned,
aside from sore knees, I seemed fine.

Now when my doctor asks me if I have fallen
in the last year, at my next appointment,
I will have to say yes—or lie.

An Old Greek Statue

My nephew asks me a month ago, or is it a year now,
when he was talking about his faith and my apparent lack,
what I would do if when I die, I discover he was right
about God. He openly calls for a theocracy in America.

Hold my ground for as long as I can, I answer.
He grins at me with the grin of those who know.
It's an old Job question in a way, this struggle between
good and evil in the face of cosmic indifference.

I use the word "good" as if it represents
something real and not just a social construction
to grease the machinery. I believe in the good,
I tell him. But without God, my nephew offers.

This morning I play ballistics with kettlebells.
I remind myself that even as an old man,
I am developing skills, this playing with chunks
of iron. I am learning to fire muscles in sequence:

one arm alternating swings, inside circles,
outside circles, around the leg cleans, snatches.
I think in kilograms not pounds—all to challenge
the brain to keep learning.

I am waging a losing battle, I know.
When face to face with God, Job realizes
he is just a worm. Jesus cries out from the cross,
"why have you forsaken me."

Amanda tells Marx Marvelous that there is no meaning
to life. But there is style, she says. There is the snatch,
swinging the bell up and posing with it straight
above your head as if you were an old Greek statue.

Gray Mornings

1 *The Bull*

I am a boy—I don't remember how old—
walking an Arkansas field with men
carrying shotguns.

Two uncles, my grandfather,
my father.
They give me an unloaded .22
rifle to carry.

A bull shows itself in the mist,
in the field. It trots toward us.
The men bend the wires of a fence
and scramble through.

I on the other hand stand my ground,
shouldering my empty gun.
Someone reaches over the fence
and lifts me in one easy motion.

The men laugh.

2 *We sailed from San Juan*

We dock in New York
after six days
on the brooding Atlantic.

Somewhere off the Carolina coast,
we watch flying fish
jet from the ship's wake
and skirt the Ocean surface.
Look!

We stop in Cuba
for a day—
four years before Fidel.

My father smuggles a case of rum
from the island where we lived
for three years.

      3   *Stateside*

I am unaccustomed to the cold.
My eyes burn.

      4   *Coffee*

Coffee becomes a gray morning sacrament—
hot and black.

We sit at a table in the union
and talk about the world
unfolding before us,

as if we were integral
to the narrative,
as if we knew things.

Forty-five years later, Bob and I
sit at a table in Central Market
and talk about Kinneavy—
how he spent all those years
in a monastery
reading in original languages.
Greek, Latin, French, German—

    5 *Earth*

I stand barefoot in the grass
wrapped in my jacket
on a cold misty Saturday morning.

I am no longer interested
in teaching or building houses.

I try to feel the rotation
of the Earth through the soles
of my feet.

Real

The dying live oaks in front of my house
are old characters in my personal narrative.
They cling to life.

We have trimmed away the dead limbs,
the trees like beggars now with arms stretched
up toward the sky.

Rest my cheek against the bark of one.
Close my eyes and imagine myself with roots
growing deep.

Spend my idle time during the pandemic
buying online things I need or want,
want being a tricky word.

I use my new folding knife to open a box
of low sugar chocolates received in the mail,
the sharp blade doing its job.

Write in my journal with a recently purchased
fountain pen, as if the fountain pen
were closer to being real.

I take delight in the ink stains on my fingers.
A way of hanging on, a way of saying
all this matters.

Love and Avocados

I can tell you about love and avocados,
the poet says as they wait for drinks and appetizers.
But first, I must tell you about the *puma rosa,*
a fruit so delicate it must be eaten from the tree,
so delicate that even the name is a mystery.

They lived on the island, when they were boys,
in the tropics between the Atlantic and the Caribbean Sea
where the sun was bright and warm even in December,
and where they would spend much of their time
hanging from limbs, crawling from branch to branch,

searching out the fruit, shifting from pink to purple,
a slight of hand trick, a transformation,
when bitter became sweet if only for a moment.
Picking the fruit and eating it while dangling
above the ground in the canopy of a tree.

With bellies full and left to themselves,
the boys would gather on opposite sides of a road
and hurl rocks at each other. It was only game,
a boy's game, choosing sides
and hurling rocks seemed a natural thing.

As natural as the tadpoles raining from the sky,
appearing by the thousands in ditches and puddles.
The boys would gather a few and put them in jars
and watch them grow into tiny frogs, feeding them bread
and smaller tadpoles from more recent rains.

As natural as the baseball they played year-round.
I was left-handed, the poet says. We only had
right-handed gloves. Right-handed gloves fit
on the left hand in baseball, but that seemed right,
and I became good at catching and switching.

Catching and switching…the poet repeats the phrase.
The world was round, and everything seemed right.
God was looking down, and we prayed to him at night
for roller skates and baseballs and souls to take
if we should die before we wake.

He pauses. No one seems to know the *puma rosa*.
We mention it to people from the island,
and they give us a puzzled look. We describe
the little red pear, red only being a transition color.
They shrug and shift the talk to avocados.

Why avocados instead of mangos or bananas
is another mystery. But there it was, the avocado
growing in the tree just outside our door.
One night my father, coming home
with the sweet smell of an old war on his breath,
whipped me for refusing to eat one.

Whipped him with a strap and explained with logic bent
that avocados grew wild here and should be appreciated.
Grew wild and free here. On the mainland they were dear,
and he would understand someday, repeating the old refrain,
one he never learned to properly revere.

I was a boy and had yet to develop a taste
for the fruit, he explains in simple terms.
I also never really understood the wisdom hidden
in the lessons taught with a strap.
I still remember the sting though.

And the sting of the rock.
Was it then that the world changed?

Or was it when one of the twins, the pretty one he thinks,
though he could never tell them apart, pulled him aside
after play rehearsal and led him from the dark theatre
into the sunlight behind the building and told him.

Searching his eyes with hers, searching his eyes with hers,
stumbling on the words for the first time,
casting spells on the moment for the first time.
Did she know?

The rock hit its mark, and blood gushed from an open wound.
The boys all fled, leaving him there
frozen for a moment between worlds.
I still have the scar, the poet tells them,
touching a spot on his forehead.

He looked at her, not knowing what to do.
They were only eight, or were they nine?
Rehearsing for a Christmas play
with wise men and angels.
The December sun bright and warm.

I love you, she told him,
not knowing she was merely rehearsing.
He hesitated for a moment between worlds
and then kissed her on the cheek,
not knowing what else to do.

I can tell you about love and avocados, the poet says
as they waited for drinks and appetizers.
But I'm not sure it would make any sense.
Still, I believe in love.

He pauses and almost sighs. And I like avocados
now that I have to pay for them.

Notes, references, and allusions to other works

"An Invitation"—The meeting between Thomas Merton and Czeslaw Milosz in a San Francisco restaurant is the focus of Angela O'Donnell's poem "The Conversation" in *Saint Sinatra and other poems*.

"I Come Here Often, He Says"—The Rilke line about beauty is from "The First Elegy." The Berryman comment about Rilke is from *Dream Songs* "3". The Brautigan scene occurs in Brautigan's *A Confederate General from Big Sur*. The ladder is a reference to Chaucer's "The Miller's Tale." The tour of Henry Miller's bathroom can be found on YouTube.

"Chopin Revisited"—The coming storm alludes to Kate Chopin's "The Storm". London Bridge is a nursery rhyme we sang as kids. Lock her up refers both to the nursery rhyme and the chants aimed at Hilary Clinton during the 2016 campaign and after.

"Sitting on the Steps of Tor House"—Tor House was Robinson Jeffers's home in Carmel, California. Erickson is Steve Erickson whose character in *The Sea Came in at Midnight* works in a "memory" hotel in Japan where clients come to her to connect to modern memory after the ancient Japanese memory had been annihilated by the West after the war. Virginia is Virginia Woolf.

"Rainy Day Reading"—Crusoe's tiny volcanos refer to Elizabeth Bishop's poem "Crusoe in England." Bishop's note to her class is found on page 637 of *One Art*.

"An English Garden"—Bret Foster was the author of *The Garbage Eater* and *Fall Run Road*.

"Ada"—The two Elizabeth Bishop poems referred to in this poem are "In the Waiting Room" and "Crusoe in England."

"Another Day, Another Dollar"—The comments by the El Paso judge and the Texas Lt. Governor were reported in the news by various outlets.

"The Resistance"—Town Lake in Austin, Texas is now called Lady Bird Lake.

"Prophecies"—Augusto César Sandino was a Nicaraguan rebel leader who fought the U.S. marines from 1927 to 1933. The Brautigan story is "Homage to the San Francisco YMCA" in *Revenge of the Lawn*.

"Everything Happens Here"—Hans is Hans Castorp, the main character in Thomas Mann's *The Magic Mountain*. The 400-pound man sitting in the basement of his home was an imagined character in the mind of a future president of the United States.

"Reading Angela"—refers to Angela O'Donnell's "St. Clarence" in her *Saint Sinatra and other poems*.

"Legacy"—Hank in this poem is Charles Bukowski.

"Like Breath"—Gertz is Sandee Gertz, author of *The Pattern Maker's Daughter*. Hall is Donald Hall.

"Not Such a Long Time Anymore"—I believe I read the story about Lincoln's second inauguration in *The Texas Reader* when I was working on a bibliographical checklist of textbooks published for the Confederate Schools, but I can't find a copy to confirm it. Edna is Edna Pontellier in Kate Chopin's *The Awakening*. I took liberties with the timeline and her encounter with Castro. Most readers believe she died somewhere in the Gulf.

"A Christmas Carol"—The movie scene from *The Godfather* of course.

"Something We Miss"—Jane Kenyon's poem "Mud Season".

"The Apple"—The James Baldwin reference is to the essay "Stranger in the Village". I taught that essay over a span of thirty years. Never did get it right.

"The Billboard Baby"—The Billboard Baby used to be next to IH-10 just west of Phoenix, Arizona. It was moved during the reconstruction of the highway years ago.

"Brown Wasps"—The reference to Loren Eiseley is to his essay "The Brown Wasps". I also taught that essay for thirty years, but I think I got that one right. My students started telling me toward the end that I mainly liked to teach "old man" essays.

"Using a Whetstone"—Refers to Robert Pirsig's *Zen and the Art of Motorcycle Maintenance*.

"Napalm in the Morning"—HEB is a Texas grocery store chain, and like all things Texan, people in the state never cease to brag about it. It should be noted that their store brand ice cream is competitive with the best.

"Tis the Season"—Refers to Carolyn Forche's poem "The Colonel" in *The Country Between Us*.

"We Live in Seclusion"—I was reading a series of essays online when I came across the term bradykinin storm and the notion that your lungs can turn to Jell-O. I wasn't taking notes and don't remember the source for this information. Sally Ball's poem "Slope" is in her book *Annus Mirabilis*. It is one of my favorite books of poetry.

"What We Do"—Here we find another reference to the Nicaraguan guerilla fighter Sandino. Dancing to the music of Clifton Chenier is a line in Paul Simon's song "That Was Your Mother" in the album *Graceland*. I want you green is from García Lorca's poem "Sleepwalking Ballad". The connection between Duke Ellington and the notion of the true meaning of democracy is made in Stanley Crouch's sermon "Premature Autopsies."

"A Dream World"—The Canto is one of Ezra Pound's. The banker is T.S. Eliot.

"Miscellaneous Jazz"—The Brautigan comment about the Pacific Ocean and Monterey, California comes from the short story "Pacific Radio Fire" in *Revenge of the Lawn*.

"An Old Greek Statue"—The sentiments of Amanda come from *Another Roadside Attraction* by Tom Robbins.

"Gray Mornings"—Kinneavy is James Kinneavy, author of *A Theory of Discourse*.

Brady Peterson lives near Belton, Texas. He is the author of *Glued to the Earth, Between Stations, Dust, From an Upstairs Window,* and *García Lorca is Somewhere in Produce.*

www.ingramcontent.com/pod-product-compliance
Lightning Source LLC
Chambersburg PA
CBHW020942090426
42736CB00010B/1232